Why this book?

As a church minister I count it as one of the greatest
privileges in my life when I am invited to speak at or take
a lead of some sort at a funeral service. I always feel
honoured to be asked to pay tribute to someone's life in this
way and to be trusted to convey some words that will hopefully
help. I try to find words and prayers which might help people
give thanks for the life they knew, continue to mourn for the loss
they have experienced and to reflect on the implications for their
own lives. I pray hard that some of the words will be particularly
poignant and appropriate and helpful.

Whenever I have done this I have also felt that there are some
further words that I am not supposed to say yet. This might be
because they don't fit in the time we have for a service, but it is
more likely that they are words which fit best at another time,
some words to store away and look at later.

For some, this 'other time' might be the same day as the funeral
service, later in the evening when things have quietened down.
For many these words might be more helpful weeks or months
later.

The words in this short book represent a collection of thoughts
designed to be these words for another time.

They come from listening and talking to people who have known the loss of a close relative or friend. They also come from my own experience of this type of loss. My experience of funerals and bereavement is not just as the person at the front - I have had my share of sitting with others in the chairs or pews whilst others lead a service for one of my loved ones.

> Death and bereavement affect us all. It is one of the things we genuinely share in common.

Death and bereavement affect us all. It is one of the things we genuinely share in common.

And yet, when it comes to the death of a loved one and bereavement we are also all different.

My hope is that somewhere in the pages that follow there will be some words which will be helpful to you. Which page precisely? I don't know, because we are all different. There are seven key thoughts. Feel free to ignore anything in this book if it isn't helpful - if one page isn't "scratching where you itch" then try the next one.

At the end I have shared a little bit of my own experience, and also offered some verses, a prayer, and some links to further sources of help.

There are **no rules**

There

I once asked a doctor friend if some symptoms I was experiencing were possibly a side effect from a new medicine I had to take. He said that in his experience he had come to the conclusion that if people had a new set of symptoms that weren't normally part of their lives then it was logical to at least first consider that they might be a result of the new medicine.

With loss and bereavement I've noticed something similar. If you are experiencing some new feelings, something that is different, something that has changed in your mood, things being harder, then consider that it might be a symptom of loss. Just as we all experience different symptoms for common illnesses, your symptoms may be different to those of other people.

There has been much written about possible experiences as the result of grief, and different recognised stages of grief too. We don't all fit these stages or templates. Common experiences can include sorrow, pain (even physical pain), loneliness, depression, anger, denial, unusually vivid dreams, or a sense that life has lost its meaning. It can change how we relate to others, make us restless, disorganised, irritable. Some people want to talk a great deal about the deceased person. There are many other 'symptoms' besides.

There can be great comfort in knowing that the way that you are feeling is to be expected and that many other people who have lost a loved one have felt the same way.

There is great strength in that, but there are no checklists. There are no stages you must go through, or feelings you ought to have. The bottom line is simply that we are all different and that the feelings and issues we experience and the timing of those feelings and issues are all different too.

Some people will need a considerable amount of time away from work; others won't. If we are in a very 'face to face' or caring profession this can also add extra pressure.

Shared experiences and empathy from others who understand can be very helpful but where they aren't please don't add to your sorrow by feeling bad that your feelings don't fit.

Remember too that everyone approaches grief with their own cultural perspective, whether they realise it or not. It is worth recognising when you have been at a funeral with people from different countries or cultural backgrounds.

There can be great comfort in knowing that the way that you are feeling is to be expected and that many other people who have lost a loved one have felt the same way.

I have Sri Lankan and British relatives, and in some ways they deal with loss and bereavement totally differently. My Sri Lankan relatives would come to the home of the person most closely linked to the person who has died, often with food that is culturally associated with these occasions, and just sit for hours, with no need to say anything. For me personally, I found that something I needed to adjust to. British people on the whole tend to want to know how they can help. They love to have a role which means they are contributing to the need. It helps them to feel, and be, valuable in that situation.

Also, almost every other country in the world arranges the funeral quicker than we do in Britain. This will be more helpful for some than for others. In the UK, planning a funeral has become increasingly pressurised, with expectations of stories, pictures etc. It can be simple or complicated, neither is right or wrong.

In fact none of these differences are right or wrong. They are just different ways of dealing with things.

There are no rules

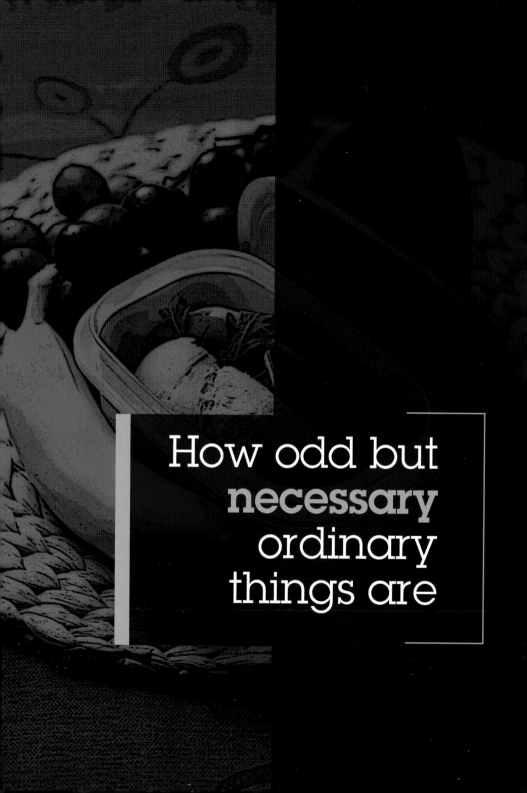

How odd but
necessary
ordinary
things are

How odd but **necessary** ordinary things are

The actress Susan Sarandon was once interviewed about her film 'Dead Man Walking', about people facing a death sentence, and how she had processed that.

She said:

"At my most vulnerable what I fear most is leaving the children before I know they are happy and I know they are safe. But actually, it's good to have to think about death. Death's what's real in life. It's just that we find ways to be busy. If we lived every day with death we would live a different life and it would not necessarily be a depressing one. It would probably be more joyful.

You know, I often lose the ability to prioritize. I'm rushing to get lunch for the children and put the toilet paper on the toilet paper thing and read the scripts and it takes a kid getting sick or something to remember that it's not so important that there is stuff all over the floor; maybe you should play with your kids. People say that if we think about death all the time we'd go mad but maybe we'd go sane."

"People say that if we think about death all the time we'd go mad but maybe we'd go sane."

Sometimes in the middle of grief, while this massive loss has happened to us, it just feels odd that ordinary mundane things continue.

We watch other people carry on with jobs and relationships and meals and shopping and even fun things and entertainment and it can all feel quite odd, as though these normal things simply don't fit the way that we are feeling.

And yet those ordinary things do continue and they must continue. People must carry on and we must carry on. Resumption of normal life in some form is an aim for those who are grieving. Even though they might feel strange, we need to carry on eating, drinking, talking, walking and working and all the regular things that we fill our life with. In the strangeness, it can even help us in picking up the pieces again. In due course we need to prepare a meal, make the tea, have regular conversations that aren't to do with preparing a funeral or dealing with all the paperwork that follows after someone dies.

Sometimes these things take longer and require more energy than normal. It is just good to know that this is a common phenomenon and not add to our guilt by wondering why the simple things take so much longer. Often they just will.

But there's also an opportunity here.

Because we have experienced this huge loss, when we come back to them we may find that some of the things we fill our lives with haven't been so important after all. Perhaps they could benefit from a bit of reassessment. There is an opportunity to look again at our priorities with a fresh perspective, and work out what really is important. There is a balance there somewhere, between getting back to normal life, and looking at it again with new eyes.

If only

If only

I recently read an interview with a well known writer of fiction. He was asked where he got his ideas, and answered: 'You get ideas when you ask yourself simple questions … and one important question to ask is "if only…" so you can imagine life another way.'

I got the distinct impression that the 'if only' questioning process for this author doesn't make things easy, but it is helpful, and ultimately a worthwhile thing to think through and work through.

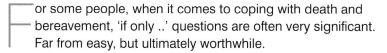

or some people, when it comes to coping with death and bereavement, 'if only ..' questions are often very significant. Far from easy, but ultimately worthwhile.

There are two very different sorts of 'if only…' which we typically ask after a close friend or relative has died.

The first is all about wishing we'd said or done something differently.

When I have conducted funerals I often use one or two prayers that are somewhat more scripted than the way I would normally pray in a church service. One prayer which has been helpful for people has focused on the 'if only' we feel when we wish we'd said or done something. This prayer is below, but first it is worth saying two things:

Firstly, we can all pray, even if we are not used to praying. It is an option available to everyone and we can find strength in that.

Secondly, it is important to remember that it is not about what we did or did not say in those last moments. It is not about being there in the last moment. It is about the sum total of our relationship.

Even if that relationship wasn't as it should have been and had broken down, my belief is that God can help us there too in what can otherwise add difficulty and grief. This is the prayer I pray in a funeral service. When I conducted my first funeral service the senior Minister I was working with, Ian White, offered these words to me for inclusion in the service and I have found them helpful ever since. I understand that Ian's father wrote them:

"Should there be any feelings of regret that we failed to do or say some things -

grant us your forgiveness

grant healing where there is hurt

grant trust where there is doubt

grant hope where there is sadness

Then in your great mercy, give us faith so that we can face the future with confidence, trusting in God.

We ask it in the name of our Lord Jesus Christ   Amen"

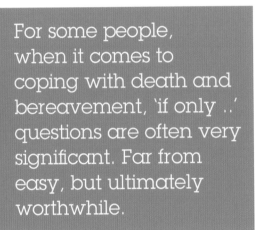

For some people, when it comes to coping with death and bereavement, 'if only ..' questions are often very significant. Far from easy, but ultimately worthwhile.

There is a second 'if only'. It is what many of us feel after particularly difficult deaths or traumatic ones – the death of a child, for example. The 'if only' that we cry out to God. 'If only that person had been saved', 'If only they hadn't died'. In effect we are asking God, 'Why?'

I wish I could offer a straightforward answer here. I am afraid that I can't, but what I can say is that we find resonance with the 'if only' prayers that are there in the Bible. And from that I learn that God is more than happy to receive those 'if only' questions personally. All I know about the totality of the character of God as found in the Bible, is that what we currently see, in terms of difficulty and death, isn't God's first or ultimate solution and that there is a bigger plan to come.

If you do have either or both of these 'if onlys', then know that they are part of the pattern for very many of us. I know of nowhere else to take either set of 'if onlys' – our personal ones about what we should have said or done, or the ones directed at God confused about what happened - but to God himself. I am convinced that it doesn't do us any good to pretend that these issues are not there and all that I know about God has taught me that he is more than happy to receive our honest 'if onlys'.

If only

Tides and
waves

I remember going to see a play a few weeks or months after my Dad had died. It wasn't a great play to be honest, and yet at one point in it I found myself in tears simply because one of the actors walked with a very stumbling and difficult walk which looked like my Dad's way of walking when he was very, very ill.

This was a flashback moment. It was a caught-by-surprise moment.

I hadn't prepared for it.

When we have lost somebody we often prepare ourselves for things we are going to feel on key dates and anniversaries, the birthdays, the wedding anniversaries, the anniversary of the death itself. They can be hugely sad occasions but sometimes we build up a kind of resistance to them.

At the same time, we are less prepared for things that just catch us by surprise, particularly in the early days, weeks, or months, but it could happen at any stage.

Tides and **waves**

So, for example, we are watching a TV programme, and it can seem as though almost every programme that we watch suddenly reminds us of the person we have lost, or is about death. We are not prepared for that. Or someone speaks to us and something in their character or words takes us back. Or we are making tea and we suddenly realise that we have made two cups of tea and not one, because we have made one for the person that we lost. We have been caught by surprise.

Suddenly, very early on, not saying 'she likes this' or 'he loves that', but rather 'she liked this' or 'he loved that'.... that simple act of finding ourselves needing to use the past tense about the person we've lost can catch us by surprise.

When we have lost somebody we often prepare ourselves for things we are going to feel on key dates and anniversaries

Those things may be more trivial than the anniversaries but they can hurt even more, I think, perhaps because we can't build up a defence mechanism against them. If you experience this, it is part of the grieving process. Don't be surprised when you are caught by surprise.

C. S. Lewis talked about the symptoms of grief coming in waves and I think that's right. The tide is something you can predict. It comes with certain timings. You can even buy a timetable. Sometimes we prepare ourselves as though the symptoms of grief are going to come like the tide, where we can predict what comes next. But waves.... waves are much less predictable and you don't know when the next big one is going to come and hit you.

Tides and waves

Help from
others

C.S. Lewis talking about his own bereavement after the death of his wife in his book, *A Grief Observed*, said:

There is a sort of invisible blanket between the world and me. I find it hard to take in what anyone says or perhaps hard to want to take it in. It is so uninteresting. Yet I want the others to be about me. I dread the moments when the house is empty. If only they would talk to one another and not to me.

Help from others

There is the sense here that many of us feel at times, that even if people don't say anything very significant or important - sometimes it is enough that they are there.

There is huge value in people helping us with practical issues. There is equally great value in people who listen. There is also a warning that some who offer answers for the difficult questions aren't helping if those answers are offered too glibly and too quickly. They may mean well, but sometimes they may really just be trying to help themselves feel a bit better. If somebody offers you 'helpful' words and they are not helpful to you then you don't have to accept them as words that are right for you.

There are times when being with others might feel strange, but is part of what we need. We are relational people.

And yet, despite the weakness sometimes in the words of others, we need other people and we need to recognise their value in helping us through the process. There are times when being with others might feel strange, but is part of what we need. We are relational people. Grief is something that we share in common. Almost none of us escape it unless we die too soon to have experienced it. Other people help us through the process.

Some people are stuck in grief, deep grief, for too long, and need another kind of help. If you wonder whether this is you, please consider seeking specialist help, perhaps counselling. Your GP might be a first port of call, or your minister or pastor if you are connected with a church. Please feel no guilt in availing yourself of that kind of support. If in the longer term you are finding it hard to just 'keep on keeping on' – to carry on with the normal run of things in life then that's a sign that we need help – and help is out there and a better way forward can be found.

There is a list of some possible sources of help at the end of this book.

The **stop asking** time

The **stop asking** time

Queen Elizabeth the Queen Mother was asked some years after losing her husband if the pain of the loss gets better with time. She said: "I'm not sure if it gets any better, but we get better at it."

For many of us, the Queen Mother's words are more honest than the standard answer that 'time is a great healer'. But, nevertheless, time does help us to process, and we do get better at dealing with the reality of what we've experienced.

As a minister of a church I am involved with many people who have gone through loss and bereavement. One common experience, I've noticed, is that friends stop asking how we're doing after a while. At first, everyone seems keen to know how we are, and that is great. Then all of a sudden, as if by some unspoken agreement, they all seem to stop. It's as if they all decided that we don't want to talk about it any more, so they all stop asking. Or at least it feels like that.

In the early days when we are bombarded by 'how are we doing' questions, we may well not be ready for them.

The point at which they all seem to stop asking varies. For an older person where the death was more expected it is sooner. For a younger person where the death was more of a shock it can take longer until that point where it seems everyone uncannily stops asking and moves on. They may well mean no harm by their silence (they may well mean the best by it) but it can seem like they don't care or have underestimated our loss.

The irony is that in the early days when we are bombarded by 'how are we doing' questions, we may well not be ready for them. Then, later on when people feel that bringing the subject up in conversation won't be what you want, the reverse can be true – we might really welcome one person, one good friend who is willing to go on asking, to go on listening.

If you recognise that this could happen or has happened then what I would hope and pray for you is that you would have at least one good friend and you can agree with them that they and you can go on talking about your loss later, when others have stopped because the process of grieving goes on. It may not be as intense but it goes on.

The **stop asking** time

The **reflection**
time

The **reflection** time

We live in a time when it can seem as though 'death' is the new taboo that should not be mentioned. The Victorians had sex and money as their taboo subjects, but seem to have talked about death all of the time. We almost live in reverse: it is sex and money that dominate conversations in the media, they are the trendy subjects to discuss. It can seem as though we are not supposed to talk about death.

Something about death shines a light on some things that we can so easily keep dark.

In the midst of processing loss and bereavement there is an opportunity.

Consider three perspectives in how we relate to loss:

There is me and my personal thoughts and feelings about the one I have lost.

There is me and my thoughts about the others involved in the loss – perhaps the other family or friends who have been impacted, those who are left. How the relationships may have changed.

And finally, there is me and God.

My observation is simply this. In order for our grieving process to be complete – for it to be all that it can be - we need to consider each of those three aspects. I often see people processing just two of these things, and it is not enough.

So, some people seem to neglect the first aspect. They are so quick to be concerned for how others are doing, and perhaps so strong and assured in their belief in God and the promise of eternity that they don't allow themselves personally to grieve.

Others think about the person they have lost and God and don't see a need for other people. I've tried to explain elsewhere why we desperately need others as well.

But many try to bypass God. Their grieving process is just about the person they have lost and the others that are left. This is a very great shame, because something key is missing if we do this.

It can seem as though we are not supposed to talk about death.

Something about death shines a light on some things that we can so easily keep dark.

Most of the time in our lives there is a danger that we don't think through and talk through the big issues. Life and death are very high on the list of big issues, and any death can make other issues which normally occupy our heads seem inconsequential. This isn't necessarily a bad thing.

The plea that I am making is that there are these three perspectives in our grief, and unless we attend to all three something vital is missing.

We can both mourn and give thanks for the one we have lost in a personal way, sometimes at the same time because there is no contradiction between them.

We can also focus on our relationship with other people, how we need that, how it may have changed, how it may need extra work now.

And thirdly, we can think about our relationship with God. As I mentioned earlier, something about death shines a light on some things that we can so easily keep dark. That is useful. It helps us to consider our own mortality and where we stand. There is an opportunity there and it is for each of us to take it.

You may find the prayer below one way to help consider all three aspects.

A **prayer** to pray

Lord I am thinking again now of the person I knew and loved, the person whose life on earth has ended.

I think of all that was good in their life, seen and unseen things, and I thank you for them. Thank you that the positive effects of the good things they did can continue.

At the same time I also mourn for the loss I experience now. I mourn because they are no longer here. Please help me in my grieving. Please help me to see no contradiction in both being thankful and mourning at the same time, for the same person.

Lord I am also thinking now of my friends and family. I thank you for them. Help us to go on thinking of the person we have lost. Help us to go on freely telling the stories that come to mind. Help us to go on supporting each other.

Lord God I am thinking now about you. Please help me to place my trust in you and find help and hope there.

Thank you that Jesus conquered death and therefore that there is hope for all of us.

Lord, through Jesus, please forgive me for the wrongs in my past. Help me through the issues I face today and lead me into the future, even into eternity with you.

Thank you

Amen

A bit about **my own** experience

On the day I got married my father died.

On the morning of my wedding day I was staying at my parents' house. I was shaving and my mum called me and said, "I think he's gone". My dad had cancer, and we had known for months that it was possible he may not make it to the wedding. We went ahead with the wedding that day anyway, as he would have wanted, and we changed the best man's humorous speech to something that felt more appropriate and then my wife, Sue, and I stayed around until the funeral a week or so later. A friend at church realised that we wouldn't be going to our honeymoon, and booked a hotel for us for that time. That was really needed, very significant for us, just to get away for a few days.

I learned a whole range of things in those circumstances. Sue and I had already been learning about bereavement, because in the six months during which we were engaged, Sue's dad died quite unexpectedly one night from a heart attack. So, having wondered whether my dad would make it to the wedding or not, we always assumed her dad would and in the end neither did.

Now, looking back, I don't count myself as having suffered greatly at all. I have a great marriage and would much rather have that than a particularly smooth wedding day. But I learned some of the things that I wanted to say in this book. One of the things I found least helpful was people providing glib answers, so I have tried not to do that here.

I used to think that my first question in heaven would be why my dad died when he did. I don't think that now. I still don't know why it happened the way it did, but I know it has affected the way I do my job. Some people through their love and character and actions conveyed the love of Jesus to me - in the time when I needed help. One of the things that I valued most was people just being there.

It can take time for us to look back on events from the perspective of others involved. It took me time to see things from my mum's perspective. I remember a minute or two of just pure anguish from her at the point of realising my dad had died, and then

> I learned a whole range of things in those circumstances. Sue and I had already been learning about bereavement.

from that point onwards she just continued on amazingly and has done ever since, and a lot of my thoughts on mourning and bereavement come from her. It's taken me a long while to realise that. I am an only child, and in a way on that day she lost both of us, because I was leaving home to start a married life, and on the same day she lost her husband. How difficult that must have been for her.

Another memory I have of that day was when two vans, almost identical in make and model, arrived at the family house. One of them was the florist van coming to deliver the wedding flowers. The other was the private ambulance to collect my dad's body. They pulled up at the same time as I came out of the house. The two drivers looked at each other. Working out what they both were - just the incongruity of it – I realised that this was new ground for everybody, and it was okay to be lost because these two professional people were lost for words too.

There is something else that I should say: the last thing that my dad did on this earth is pray with my mum that morning as he did every morning. I take huge strength from that. I'm sure that in his list of prayers he prayed for my marriage and for my life and for all that would follow and I still continue to benefit from that.

Many people have found some of the most important words for another time are found in the Bible.

I keep my eyes always on the Lord. With him at my right hand, I shall not be shaken.
Psalm 16:8

He has made everything beautiful in its time. He has also set eternity in the human heart; yet no one can fathom what God has done from beginning to end.
Ecclesiastes 3:11

The Lord upholds all who fall and lifts up all who are bowed down.
Psalm 145:14

Praise be to the God and Father of our Lord Jesus
Christ, the Father of compassion and the God of all
comfort, who comforts us in all our troubles, so that we
can comfort those in any trouble with the comfort we
ourselves receive from God.
2 Corinthians 1:3-4

My soul is in deep anguish. How long, Lord, how long?
Psalm 6:3

I lift up my eyes to the mountains – where does my help
come from?
My help comes from the Lord, the Maker of heaven and
earth.
Psalm 121:1-2

'Do not let your hearts be troubled. You believe in God;
believe also in me. My Father's house has many rooms;
if that were not so, would I have told you that I am
going there to prepare a place for you? And if I go and
prepare a place for you, I will come back and take you
to be with me that you also may be where I am.'
John 14:1-3

Jesus answered, 'I am the way and the truth and the
life. No one comes to the Father except through me.'
John 14:6

If you prayed the prayer in this book or if you would like to know more, you might like to consider:

talking with the person who gave this to you

visiting www.christianity.org.uk

writing to Christian Enquiry Agency
Freepost WC2947
South Croydon
CR2 8UZ

looking for a course which gives space to explore the big questions of life. Look for a local Alpha course **www.alpha.org** or a local Christianity Explored course **www.christianityexplored.org**

Bereavement support can also be found through Cruse, **www.crusebereavementcare.org.uk**